HEINEMANN Profiles

Adolf Hitler

Richard Tames

First published in Great Britain by
Heinemann Library
Halley Court, Jordan Hill,
Oxford OX2 8EJ
a division of Reed Educational and
Professional Publishing Ltd.
Heinemann is a registered trademark of
Reed Educational & Professional
Publishing Limited.

OXFORD MELBOURNE
AUCKLAND KUALA LUMPUR
SINGAPORE IBADAN NAIROBI
KAMPALA JOHANNESBURG
GABORONE PORTSMOUTH NH
CHICAGO

Designed by Visual Image, Taunton.
Printed in Hong Kong / China

Details of written sources:
Bullock, Alan, *Hitler and Stalin: Parallel
Lives*, HarperCollins, 1991; Laing, Stuart,
The Illustrated Hitler Diary 1917–1945,
Marshall Cavendish, 1980; Neville, Peter,
Life in the Third Reich, B T Batsford, 1992;
Tames, Richard, *Nazi Germany*, B T
Batsford, 1985; Wistrich, Robert, *Who's
Who in Nazi Germany*, Weidenfeld and
Nicolson, 1982.

02 01 00
10 9 8 7 6 5 4 3

ISBN 0 431 08606 0

**British Library Cataloguing in
Publication Data**

Tames, Richard, 1946–
    Adolf Hitler. – (Heinemann Profiles)
    1. Hitler, Adolf, 1889–1945 – Juvenile
    literature 2. World War, 1939–1945 –
    Biography – Juvenile literature
    I. Title
    940.5'3'088296

Acknowledgements
The Publishers would like to thank the
following for permission to reproduce
photographs: AKG Photo pp4, 15, 18, 28,
44, 46; Mary Evans Picture Library pp49,
50, 51; Imperial War Museum, London
p24; Landesbildstelle, Berlin p29; Peter
Newark's Pictures pp7, 11, 12, 13 (upper),
17, 19, 22, 31, 35, 37, 38, 48; Popperfoto
pp8, 20, 33, 43; Süddeutscher Verlag pp13
(lower, 25 (both), 26; Topsham Picture
Point p30.

Cover photograph reproduced with
permission of Barnaby's Picture Library.

Every effort has been made to contact
copyright holders of any material
reproduced in this book. Any omissions
will be rectified in subsequent printings if
notice is given to the Publisher.

Any words appearing in the text in bold,
like this, are explained in the Glossary.

CONTENTS

WHO WAS ADOLF HITLER?

Adolf Hitler was one of the most evil leaders in human history. He dreamed of making Germany the most powerful country in the world. This caused a war which cost 30,000,000 lives in Europe alone and left Germany itself divided and in ruins. Hitler's hatred of Jews, **communists** and gypsies led to the organized murder of over 6,000,000 men, women and children.

Hitler's policy in a sentence – 'One People, One Realm, One Leader'.

Ein Volk, ein Reich, ein Führer!

His hatred of communism ended in communists taking over half of Europe until the 1990s.

For the first half of his life Hitler was a nobody. The few people who knew him personally saw him as a failed artist who crazily believed he would one day be famous and powerful. Hitler had neither education nor wealth, had never travelled abroad and spoke only German. Yet he convinced himself and, later, millions of others that he was a master of world politics and could lead Germany to a glorious future.

After Hitler's adopted country, Germany, was defeated in World War I, its people gave way to disorder and despair. This enabled Hitler to use **propaganda** and violence to present himself as the leader Germany needed to wipe out its shame and become proud and strong again. For years it seemed to his adoring followers as though Hitler would succeed brilliantly at everything he did. But the 'Greater Germany' he tried to create by war was based on **plundering** Europe and turning its peoples into slaves. When Germany at last faced defeat he ordered its total destruction and shot himself in the wreckage of Berlin, which he had sworn to make the greatest city on earth.

'All propaganda ... has to adapt its ... level to the ... least intelligent ...'
Hitler in his book
Mein Kampf Vol 1 Ch 3

Childhood and Youth

A dolf Hitler was born in April 1889, not in Germany but in Austria-Hungary, a huge empire of many peoples that spread across central Europe.

Hitler grew up in and around the Austrian city of Linz. His mother, Klara, spoiled him. Of her five children, three died, leaving only Adolf and his sister Paula. Although Hitler later claimed to have been poor and badly treated as a child, this was not true. His father, Alois, was a strict, cold man. He was always telling his son off but probably for good reason. School reports described the young Adolf as lazy, disobedient and rude.

The dreamer

When Hitler became famous his admirers said he had been a natural leader at school. In fact he was more given to day-dreaming alone than playing games with friends. The only thing that seems to have interested him much were old magazines about the war of 1870–71, when Prussia and the other German states defeated France and united to form a single, great German Empire. He also liked stories about America's Wild West.

School failed to interest Hitler, but the Roman Catholic Church did. As a choirboy he was deeply impressed by its beautiful buildings and the fine

robes and music used in religious services. Twenty years later, in his book *Mein Kampf* (*My Struggle*), he would remember those childhood experiences. Dramatic parades, dashing uniforms, bold banners and solemn ceremonies were skilfully used to get people to join his **Nazi** party and become loyal to him alone.

THE IDLER

Hitler's father died in 1903. Many boys at that time had to work to help their family. But Hitler's mother had a good pension. Despite his bad reports, Hitler was able to stay on at school until he was 16. He failed to get the normal school-leaving certificate.

After leaving school he refused to get a job and was able to live off his mother. Hitler hated the idea of regular work and passed the days sketching and painting, dreaming of becoming a famous artist. He became passionate about the operas of the German composer Richard Wagner. They told stories about heroes, princesses and evil spirits from the legends of ancient Germany. Wagner was just the sort of artistic genius Hitler longed to be.

In 1907 Hitler moved to Vienna, the capital of Austria-Hungary. Twice he tried to become a student at the Academy of Fine Arts. Twice he was turned down because his pictures were not good enough. A professor advised him to try **architecture** instead.

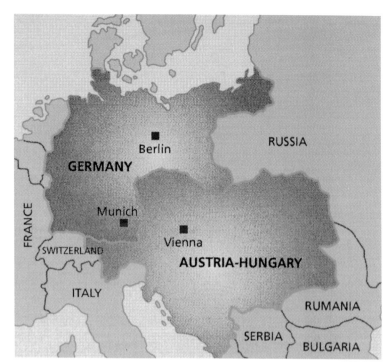

Central and Eastern Europe before 1914, showing the key cities in Hitler's life – Vienna, Munich and Berlin.

As he had no school-leaving certificate he was turned down for that course, too. But he still dreamed that a great future somehow awaited him. He even drew up elaborate plans and sketches for rebuilding Linz as though it were the magnificent capital of an empire.

THE TRAMP

With no steady work, Hitler sank into poverty, doing odd jobs, sleeping on park benches and in doorways and eating at soup kitchens for down-and-outs. But to go back to Linz would have meant admitting that he really was a failure. He was hungry and homeless but survived the winter of 1909–10. Then a fellow tramp persuaded him to paint views of Vienna, which he sold. These made enough money for Hitler to be able to move into a hostel for men, where he stayed for three years.

MAKING THE MAN

Hitler's ideas about politics were shaped by two major experiences – living in Vienna and serving as a soldier in World War I.

A VISION OF POWER

Vienna was the capital of Austria-Hungary and therefore the place for great political meetings. Hitler looked down on ordinary working people, but he did admire the strength of **trade unions**. One day he saw a parade of workers that was so long it took two hours to pass him. This convinced him that building a group of loyal, disciplined supporters was the key to personal power. At the same time he hated the **socialist** and **communist** ideas of many union leaders. Hitler scorned their claim that all humans were equal. He believed that, among both individuals and races, some were clearly better than others and had a natural right to rule over them. He also hated the idea that workers might have more in common with workers of other nations than with better-off people of their own nation. Hitler believed that the struggle of nation against nation was the key to history and that loyalty to your nation should come before everything else.

IDENTIFYING ENEMIES

Austria-Hungary was an empire of more than a dozen peoples run by officials and soldiers drawn

A German anti-Jewish poster – The Eternal Jew. It suggests the Jews were trying to bring the hammer and sickle of Soviet Communism to Germany.

from the upper classes of Austria and Hungary. Hitler was a German-speaker and looked down on people from other races and countries of the empire. He dreamed of a single state to unite all Germans as one people, with no foreigners allowed in and no Germans left out. Hitler particularly hated Jews, who made up a twelfth of the population of Vienna. Many were highly successful bankers, professors, lawyers, doctors, artists and entertainers. To most people this simply showed that they were well-educated, hard-working and talented. To Hitler, the success of many Jews proved that they were cunning deceivers of ordinary people. He thought they were plotting to cheat people through the businesses they owned, or to fool them through the books or newspapers they controlled. Eventually Hitler convinced himself that every big problem, from crime to poverty, was caused by Jews – even those who were poor themselves.

'With a suitcase ... in my hand and an unconquerable will in my heart, I set out for Vienna...I too hoped to become "something".'
Mein Kampf Vol 1 Ch 1

Hitler the soldier

In 1913 Hitler moved across the border into Germany and settled in Munich, the capital of Bavaria. But he was soon arrested for failing to sign up for military service back in Austria and was sent home. The officials released him as unfit on the grounds of 'physical weakness'.

When World War I broke out in August 1914, Hitler did join the army in Bavaria. He served as a message-runner, dashing across the battlefield under fire, carrying orders for officers. In the course of four years' service Hitler would take part in almost 40 battles. Already, by December 1914 he had been awarded a medal, the Iron Cross (Second Class), for saving the life of his superior officer. In 1916 he was wounded badly enough to be sent to hospital but later returned to the front line. In August 1918 he won the Iron Cross (First Class).

In November 1918 the war finally ended with Germany's defeat. Hitler heard the news as he lay in hospital. He had been temporarily blinded by poison gas during a battle.

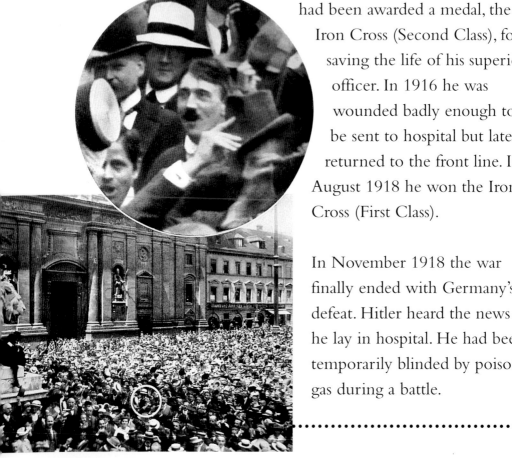

A face in the crowd, Hitler cheers the outbreak of war in 1914. Heinrich Hoffman, who took this picture, later became Hitler's personal photographer.

Hitler (top right) recovering from a wound. Army life gave him a sense of comradeship which he had never experienced before.

Hitler's fellow soldiers respected his bravery but thought him rather odd. Officers awarded him medals but never made him a sergeant, in charge of other soldiers. because they did not think him a good leader. But the war had ended the aimlessness of Hitler's life. War gave him a purpose and a sense of belonging which he had never had before.

This painting by Hitler shows the battlefield near Ypres, Belgium, where Hitler saved the life of his commanding officer.

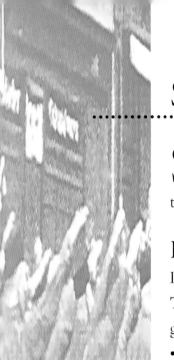

STABBED IN THE BACK!

Shortly after Germany's defeat there were **communist** uprisings in Munich and Berlin and the German empire became a **republic**.

DEFEAT AND DISGRACE

During 1919 a peace conference in Paris drew up the **Treaty** of Versailles for the new republican government to sign. Germany agreed:

- to take the blame for starting the First World War
- to pay **reparations** for war damage
- to give up lands amounting to 13 per cent of its pre-war area
- to have an army limited to 100,000 men, without tanks or big guns
- to have no submarines or airforce
- to have no troops in the Rhineland area, along its border with France
- to lose all the lands it controlled overseas.

The effects of the Versailes Treaty on Germany.

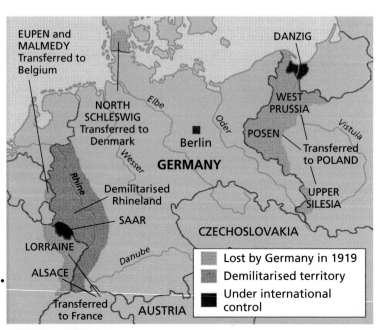

EUPEN and MALMEDY Transferred to Belgium

DANZIG

NORTH SCHLESWIG Transferred to Denmark

Elbe

Oder

Berlin

WEST PRUSSIA

Vistula

POSEN

Transferred to POLAND

Wesser

GERMANY

Rhine

Demilitarised Rhineland

UPPER SILESIA

SAAR

CZECHOSLOVAKIA

LORRAINE

Danube

ALSACE

Transferred to France

AUSTRIA

- Lost by Germany in 1919
- Demilitarised territory
- Under international control

A disabled ex-officer wears the Iron Cross while begging in the street.

BETRAYAL

Hitler was outraged by Germany's humiliation. No enemy soldier had even set foot in Germany itself. He therefore reasoned that Germany had been betrayed by enemies within, rather than beaten in battle. It was, he argued, the fault of politicians who believed in **democracy**, of **socialists** and communists and, of course, the Jews.

ENTERING POLITICS

The commanders of the defeated German army were afraid their soldiers might try to start a communist uprising like the one that had been raging in Russia since 1917, when the **Bolsheviks** seized power. All over Germany new political groups were being formed in the confusion following defeat. Many parties had their own armed guards. Trusted soldiers were ordered by the army to report on these groups and help those who were against communism. Hitler became one of the army's political agents doing this work.

The Nazi Party

The German Workers' Party (DAP) was started in Munich in January 1919 by just a few dozen people. It claimed to be against both big business and the powerful **trade unions**. It was on the side of the ordinary man in the street. In September Hitler was ordered to go to a DAP meeting. He spoke up – passionately and persuasively – impressing members so much that he was invited to join the party's main committee.

In February 1920 the DAP changed its name to become the National Socialist German Workers' Party (NSDAP) – **Nazi**, for short. Hitler was put in charge of party **propaganda**. He left the army to work full-time building up party membership.

'The broad masses of the people can only be moved by the power of speech. All great movements are popular movements. They are the volcanic eruptions of human passions and emotions, stirred either by the cruel Goddess of Distress or by the torch of the spoken word hurled among the masses.'

Mein Kampf Vol 1 Ch 3

On 11 July 1921, after a quarrel with the other leaders, Hitler left the Nazi party, declaring he would not rejoin unless he became its only leader. On 29 July a party meeting elected him sole leader. On 3 August Hitler founded a brown-shirted party guard, the **SA** (*Sturmabteilung* – Stormtrooper Unit).

This was to be used to protect speakers at public meetings, to attack **socialists** and **communists** and to parade the streets as a sign of the party's strength and discipline.

THE FIRST NAZIS

Ernst Röhm, a local army commander, was already a DAP member before Hitler joined. He was set to build up the SA. Another early member was Hermann Göring, a former fighter-pilot and national war hero. Many other recruits were ex-servicemen who admired the party's military style and welcomed its demands for loyalty, discipline and obedience, which reminded them of army life.

'SA service – pull together for Friendship, Endurance, Strength!'

MY STRUGGLE

In October 1922 Benito Mussolini, leader of the **Fascist** party in Italy, seized power by force and gradually made himself a **dictator**. Hitler believed this showed how disorder created the chance for a disciplined and determined organization to take over government and then crush all opposition to its rule.

GRASPING FOR POWER

During 1923 Germany was in crisis. Because the German government had failed to make all the **reparations** payments demanded by the Versailles **Treaty**, French and Belgian troops moved into the Ruhr industrial area and threatened to stay there until all the payments were made. German finances collapsed, making money worthless and wiping out the life savings of millions of ordinary people. **Strikes** and street-fighting added to the general feeling that the country was falling apart. Hitler was sure the time had come to act.

A German 1000-mark banknote overprinted as 1,000,000 marks. In July 1921 a US dollar exchanged for 76.7 marks and by November 1923 it was 4,200,000,000,000 marks!

On trial – Hitler and other Nazis accused of treason after the failed Munich uprising. Notice how the accused wear uniforms and medals to suggest their patriotism.

REVOLUTION AND PRISON

In November 1923 Hitler spoke to a packed meeting at a beer-hall in Munich. He declared that the local Bavarian government had been overthrown and that he would lead the Nazis in a march on Berlin, where they would take over the national government. They got as far as the centre of Munich, where they were stopped by police with guns. Fourteen Nazis were killed, but Hitler himself and the war-hero General Ludendorff, who marched beside him, were untouched. This became known as the Munich uprising. Hitler was tried for **treason** and sentenced to five years' imprisonment. He actually served less than a year in prison. He was allowed many visitors and used the time to write the first part of a book – *Mein Kampf (My Struggle)*. By the time of his death over 8,000,000 copies of this work had been sold or given away.

'There is no such thing as high treason against the traitors of 1918.' Hitler, in his defence speech when tried for treason in 1924.

Hitler (far left), wearing Bavarian costume, during his imprisonment in Landsberg fortress. He dictated Mein Kampf to his secretary, Rudolf Hess (second from the right).

MEIN KAMPF

Hitler's book is a mixture of history and personal memories, jumbled up with his ideas about race and politics. Hitler had no new ideas of his own but kept repeating the same basic themes over and over again:

- **Race is the key to history**. Human beings can be divided into separate races which should not be allowed to inter-breed and must remain 'pure'. The world is shaped by struggle between races. The blonde **Aryan** race is the most superior and responsible for all great human achievements. Other 'lesser' races, such as the Slavs of eastern Europe, Asians, Africans and others, only have value as slave workers for the Aryans. Jews are the lowest race and destroyers of human achievement.

- **Germany's destiny is to rule the world**. Germans are the purest type of Aryan. Germany must crush internal enemies – democrats, **communists**, Jews and others – who weaken it. Germany must expand to bring in all Germans currently living outside its borders. It must also conquer eastern Europe to provide *Lebensraum* (Living Space) where Germans can escape poverty and **unemployment** by creating ideal new Aryan communities.

- **Hitler's destiny is to make this all happen**. Parliaments and **democracy** lead to divisions, quarrels and national weakness. Germany will find unity and strength through obedience to an inspired leader (*Führer*) at the head of a disciplined movement of the nation's fittest and most loyal members. Hitler suggests himself as the *Führer*.

In his own words

Mein Kampf makes no attempt to hide Hitler's contempt for truth or the beliefs of others, as these quotations show :

'All those who are not racially pure are simply waste.'

'Only constant repeating will finally succeed in imprinting an idea on the memory of the crowd.'

'The greater the lie, the greater the chance that it will be believed.'

'Germany will either be a world power or not exist at all.'

Mein Kampf

THE PATH TO POWER

After 1924 times got better in Germany. More people found work. New money was issued which people felt they could trust. There was less violence on the streets.

MARKING TIME

The failure of the Munich uprising made Hitler think that the **Nazi** movement must work within the law for the present. This did not mean that he believed in elections, but they did offer a way to gain public attention. So the Nazis patiently built up local organizations throughout Germany, gradually getting new members.

Hitler reviewing a parade of SA men. He had a weakness for powerful cars.

They also organized spectacular party meetings to glorify Hitler as a hero-figure. In 1925 a new unit of the fittest Nazis was set up to serve as Hitler's bodyguard – the black-uniformed **SS** (*Schutzstaffel* – Protective Wing).

CRASH AND SLUMP

In October 1929 there was a collapse of confidence in businesses in America which led to a rapid fall in world trade and a banking crisis in Germany. Businesses closed down and **unemployment** soared. In such uncertain times people were much more willing to listen to leaders offering simple and extreme solutions to the crisis. Elections for Germany's *Reichstag* (Parliament) saw the Nazis become the second largest party in Germany.

PRESIDENT – OR CHANCELLOR ?

In 1932 Hitler, having only just become a German citizen officially, challenged General von Hindenburg, a hero of the First World War, for the office of President of Germany. Hindenburg won but Hitler came far ahead of any other challenger. A few months later, in new elections to the *Reichstag*, the Nazis doubled the seats they held and became the largest single party there. But elections did not create new jobs. Unemployment continued to rise. Government depended increasingly on orders approved by President von Hindenburg, rather than decisions made by the *Reichstag*.

Hitler demanded that he should be made Chancellor (Prime Minister). In secret discussions he won the backing of key politicians and businessmen. They thought that, if Hitler headed a **coalition** government in which the **Nazis** co-operated with other **conservative** parties, they could prevent him from going to extremes. In January 1933 President von Hindenburg, who deeply disliked and distrusted Hitler, nevertheless invited him to become Chancellor.

THE PRIVATE MAN

Although Hitler liked to be photographed with pretty children and surrounded by adoring women, he trusted no-one. His closest personal relationship ended in tragedy. In 1928 he rented a villa on the German–Austrian border and asked his half-sister, Angela Raubal, a daughter of his father's second marriage, to become his housekeeper. With her came her daughter, Geli, aged 17. Geli enjoyed being seen with her famous uncle. But Hitler became so jealous and possessive about her that, in September 1931, Geli shot herself. Hitler was so shocked by her death that he kept her room exactly as she had left it.

'A majority can never replace the man … . Just as a hundred fools do not make one wise man, an heroic decision is not likely to come from a hundred cowards.'
Mein Kampf Vol 1 Ch 3

Geli Raubal (left) was Hitler's ideal companion, as she did not threaten him with clever opinions of her own.

Hitler always carried a photograph of Eva Braun (right) in his wallet.

Geli's place was eventually taken by Eva Braun, an assistant to Hitler's personal photographer, Hoffman. She was determined to become Hitler's companion. In 1932 she even tried to kill herself to get his attention. It was so soon after Geli's death that Hitler thought another scandal would threaten his career and so the incident was hushed up. Although Eva became a member of Hitler's household, she was not allowed to appear with him in public and was often ignored by him in private. Forbidden to dance or smoke, and sent to her room when important guests arrived, Eva tried again to kill herself in 1935. But she stayed with Hitler to the end.

Making a Dictatorship

Within a month of Hitler becoming Chancellor, the *Reichstag* building burned down. It was later proved that a mentally ill Dutchman had done it. But Hitler declared it was the signal for an uprising and ordered mass arrests of **communists**. **SA** and **SS** men were given the powers of policemen. The first '**concentration camp**' was organized to hold political prisoners. It was claimed that people in these camps, accused of being disloyal to the **Nazi** government, could be turned into loyal Germans by healthy work and exercise. In fact they were usually beaten, starved and tortured. Often their families did not even know whether they were alive or dead.

Radio became a key tool in projecting Hitler's voice into homes, schools and factories, building an intimate link between the leader and his followers.

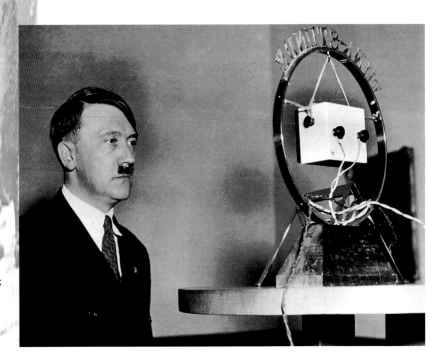

EMERGENCY!

A month after the *Reichstag* fire a law was passed
giving Hitler emergency powers for four years.
Hitler could now safely rule as a **dictator**, get rid of
non-Nazis in his government and ignore the ageing,
feeble President von Hindenburg.

CRUSHING OPPOSITION

In April 1933 a ruthless new secret police force, the
Gestapo, was set up to spy on and arrest anyone
who was against Nazism. Hitler also feared rivals
within the Nazi movement itself, especially among
leaders of the SA. Some of them believed that Hitler
really was against the power of big business. In fact
Hitler knew that he needed big business to re-arm
Germany for war. In June 1934 Hitler therefore
ordered SS units to murder SA leaders in a 'Night of
the Long Knives'. He announced that 77 plotters
had been executed for **treason**; the number actually
ran to hundreds. There were no trials, no proof – the
accusation was enough.

In August President von Hindenburg died and Hitler
declared he would become both Chancellor and
President with the title of *Führer*. A vote of all
Germans was held to approve this move, and
89.9 per cent of those voting supported it.

Persecution of the Jews

Ill-treatment of Jews began with a nationwide **boycott** of Jewish shops and businesses on 1 April 1933. A month later books by Jews, **communists** and other 'non-German' authors were publicly burned by mobs of **Nazi** students and **SA** men. In 1935 new laws banned Jews from being German citizens, or officials or teachers, or marrying '**Aryan**' Germans. Between 1933 and 1939 half of Germany's Jews left to live abroad. They included many famous writers and artists, as well as the scientist Albert Einstein. Many Germans, like Hitler, ignored the loyalty German Jews had shown during World War I – such as the Jewish officer who had recommended Hitler for the Iron Cross he proudly wore.

Re-arming Germany

Fast motorways were built to create jobs, as well as being an excellent way for moving troops quickly. The Germans secretly began to build an airforce.

An SA man (left) and SS man (right) putting up a sign saying 'Germans! Take care! Don't buy from Jews'.

Nazi propaganda map shows Germany threatened by hostile neighbours. In reality Germany had secret reserves of trained men.

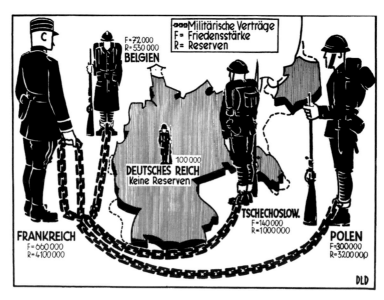

In March 1935 the German government announced it was going to re-arm and introduced a law to make all men do military training. In March 1936 Hitler went even further and sent troops into the Rhineland. All these steps had been forbidden by the Versailles **Treaty**.

German generals advised strongly against sending troops into the Rhineland, because France might send in troops against them. If they did, Germany's army would not be strong enough and would have to retreat. Hitler guessed, correctly, that France was too divided, and too afraid of another war, to do anything. And if France, with the largest army in Europe, did nothing then no other country would. Events proved him right. Many Germans felt that at last they had found a leader who would rebuild not only their nation's strength but its pride as well.

'The art of leadership consists of focusing the attention of the people on a single enemy and taking care that nothing distracts that attention.'
Mein Kampf Vol 1 Ch 3

TALKING PEACE, PREPARING FOR WAR

A SPORTING NATION

In 1936 Berlin hosted the Olympic Games. Hitler saw this as a wonderful opportunity to show off the achievements of the new **Nazi** government and the superiority of '**Aryan**' athletes. The events were very well organized. There was even closed-circuit television coverage of them, the first time this had ever been arranged. German competitors did win more gold medals than any other nation, but the star of the Games was a black American, Jesse Owens, who won four gold medals. Hitler was furious and refused to meet him.

The official poster for the 1936 Berlin Olympics features a typical 'Aryan' athlete.

In the same year the Nazi party's Hitler Youth Movement was declared to be the only legal organization for young people. Boy Scouts and other such groups were closed down and their members made to join the Hitler Youth. Sport and physical training were strongly encouraged to toughen up future soldiers, workers and mothers of 'Aryan' children.

By 1939
Nazi youth
organizations
had 7,250,000
members
aged 10–18.

MAKING ALLIES

In 1934 Hitler signed a treaty with neighbouring
Poland, agreeing that neither country would go to
war against the other. He had no intention of
keeping to this agreement but it made him look like
a man of peace.

In 1935 Hitler got the British government to agree
that Germany could have a new navy, providing it
was only a third the size of Britain's. In fact Hitler
secretly planned to build a much bigger one. In the
same year Italy invaded Ethiopia. While other powers
were against this, Hitler supported Italy. In return,
Italy became Germany's **ally**.

Civil war broke out in Spain in 1936. Both Hitler and Mussolini sent troops to help the rebel army and **Fascist** movement against the elected **socialist** government. They declared that these forces were not official but going as free individuals. In fact Hitler wanted to give his new airforce the chance to train in a real war situation.

Later that year Hitler announced that he had made another alliance, with Japan, which was trying to conquer China. Hitler claimed that the purpose of this alliance was to stop the spread of **communism**.

At a secret meeting in 1937 Hitler told the heads of the army, navy and airforce that Germany's 'problem of living space' would be settled by force by 1943 at the latest. Germany's neighbours, Austria and Czechoslovakia, were to be the first countries to be taken over.

Prosperity – for what?

In Germany, millions found new jobs. This was largely because world trade was recovering on its own, but Hitler was happy to take the credit. His main aim was to make Germany stand on its own. He wanted to prepare the country to fight using its own resources and whatever it could plunder from conquered countries. The *Volkswagen* (People's Car) was unveiled as a cheap, reliable car which most families could afford.

Hitler inspects the 'People's Car' with its designer, Ferdinand Porsche (on Hitler's left).

Workers were encouraged to join a savings plan to buy one. Their money was actually used to pay for weapons. Very few *Volkswagens* were even built until after the war because the motor industry was ordered to make trucks and tanks for the army. A cheap *Volksempfanger* (People's Radio) was, however, produced by the million – because it enabled Hitler's voice to reach into German homes, factories, schools and offices.

THE ROAD TO WAR

The situation of Jews in Germany continued to get worse. In July 1938 they were banned from working as doctors. In August they were forced to add to their existing names the name 'Israel' in the case of a man, and 'Sara' for a woman. This, in effect, made it a crime to pretend not to be a Jew. In September Jewish lawyers were banned from working. On the night of 9–10 November anti-Jewish mobs ran riot throughout Germany, burning down 177 **synagogues**, looting 7500 Jewish shops and murdering at least 91 Jews. At least 30,000 male Jews were arrested and sent to **concentration camps**.

CONQUESTS WITHOUT BLOODSHED

In February 1938 Hitler took direct command of Germany's army, navy and airforce. In March 1938 he sent German troops across the border into Austria and announced it would become a part of Germany. Austrian **Nazis** helped the takeover. Opponents were arrested.

'I pray for a defeat of my Fatherland. Only through a defeat can we atone for the terrible crimes which we have committed against Europe and the world.'

Pastor Dietrich Bonhoeffer, German conspirator against Hitler, 1943

Hitler's excuse for attacking Czechoslovakia next was that Germans living in the border area, known as the Sudetenland, were being badly treated. In September the British Prime Minister, Neville Chamberlain, met Hitler to try to avoid war. With the approval of France and Italy it was agreed that Germany should take over the Sudetenland. Czechoslovakia was not even asked to agree and, without allies, had to accept losing both the Sudetenland and its border defences. This made it easy for German troops to march into western Czechoslovakia in March 1939. The areas of Bohemia and Moravia were put under German rule while Slovakia, in the east, was allowed to become – in theory – independent. Later that month Hitler demanded that the port of Danzig and the land connecting it to Poland should be given to Germany. He also sent German troops to take over the Lithuanian port of Memel.

GOING TO THE EDGE OF WAR

Prime Minister Chamberlain saw that giving in to Hitler's demands only encouraged him to make more. Hitler clearly intended to go on adding to Germany's lands by force. In March 1939 Britain and France therefore agreed to help Poland if it was attacked by Germany.

> 'Strength lies not in defence but in attack.'
> *Mein Kampf* Vol 1 Ch 3

In August 1939 Hitler astonished the world by announcing that he had agreed with the Soviet Union (**USSR**) that neither country would go to war against the other. Hitler had always declared himself an enemy of **communism** – yet he had now made a lasting peace with the world's only communist country. In fact he had reached a secret agreement with Stalin, the Soviet leader, to divide Poland between Germany and the USSR. This meant that he could attack Poland knowing that the only country in a position to help it would not do so.

WAR

Germany went to war with Poland on 1 September 1939. Hitler claimed that Polish forces had been attacking German border posts. (Attacks had, in fact, been faked by Germany, using dead criminals and political prisoners dressed in Polish uniforms.) On 3 September Britain and France kept their promise to support Poland and declared war on Germany.

An old German
map showing
the changing
borders of
German
territory from
1938–1939.

But their armed forces were not ready to fight and there was no practical way of helping the Poles. Germany's forces used new ***Blitzkrieg*** (Lightning War) methods. They conquered Poland in a month by using fast-moving tanks and trucks of infantry, backed up by fighters and bombers.

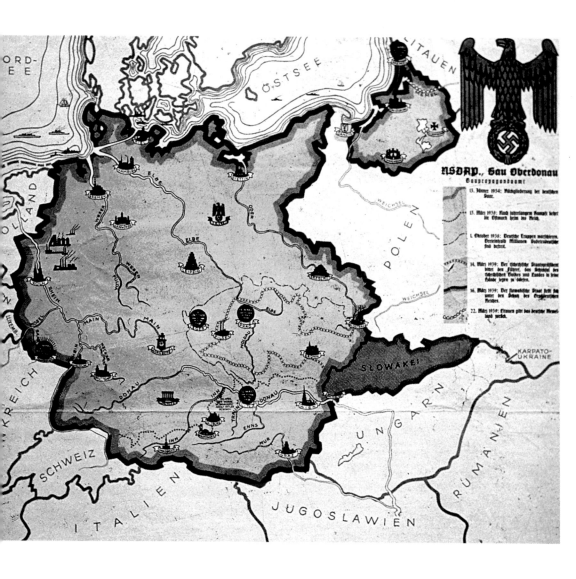

THE WARLORD

THE CONQUEST OF THE WEST

In the spring of 1940 Hitler ordered his forces to attack in the West. Between April and June they conquered Denmark, Norway, the Netherlands, Belgium, Luxembourg and France. The planned invasion of Britain depended on being able to control the skies over the English Channel. Britain's Royal Air Force defeated the German *Luftwaffe* (Air Weapon) and thus ensured that the invasion was cancelled.

Triumphant! After the defeat of France Hitler spent a day sightseeing in Paris.

SIDESHOWS

Italy was also eager to make its own conquests and in 1940 invaded Greece, but was defeated. When a pro-German government was overthrown in Yugoslavia, Germany invaded and went on to attack Greece in support of Italy. German troops were also sent to North Africa where Italian troops were fighting Britain for control. The fighting in these areas took men and machines away from the main battle zones.

BARBAROSSA

Even though Britain remained undefeated, Hitler decided in the summer of 1940 to switch his main war-making effort back to the east to achieve his long-term aims – **Lebensraum** (Living Space) for German settlement and the destruction of **communism.**

Operation Barbarossa, the invasion of the Soviet Union – with which he had previously agreed a firm peace – was launched in June 1941. Stalin, the **Soviet** leader, was simply stunned by Hitler's complete treachery in turning on him and at first Soviet forces were hopelessly disorganized. German armies raced deep into the USSR, capturing huge numbers of prisoners. But winter closed in before Moscow, the Soviet capital, could be taken. The invaders found themselves trapped in a winter war for which they were not prepared. When German generals wanted to retreat Hitler dismissed them and took personal command of the fighting.

From this time onwards, instead of setting broad aims and letting his generals work out the detailed orders, he interfered more and more himself.

'After fifteen years of work I have achieved, as a common German soldier and merely with my unbending will-power, the unity of the German nation, and have freed it from the death sentence of Versailles.' Hitler's proclamation to the troops on taking personal command, 21 December 1941

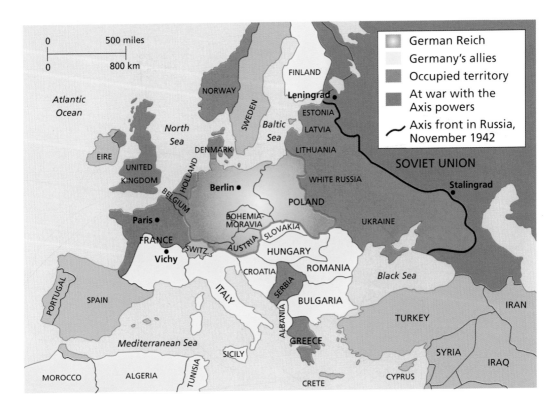

The map shows the **Nazi** conquests in 1942. This was when they were at their greatest extent.

In December 1941 Japan made a surprise attack on the US naval base at Pearl Harbor. The USA had objected to Japan's 1937 invasion of China. Japan decided that, if it was going to have to fight the USA over this, it should get in the first blow. Although this quarrel had nothing directly to do with Germany, Hitler added to his enemies by declaring war on the USA in support of his **ally** Japan. It would take time for the USA to arm and train its forces for war but Hitler had, by his own acts, now put the two most powerful states in the world against Germany.

TURNING POINTS

Until a full invasion to free Nazi-occupied Europe could be organized, the main way for Britain, the USA and their allies to fight back was by bombing.

In May 1942 Allied airforces launched the first raid of a thousand bombers, on the German city of Cologne. Bombing raids continued day and night for the next three years.

In the summer of 1942 German forces closed in on the Russian city of Stalingrad, whose defenders fought back fiercely. Then the British army in North Africa defeated the German Afrika Korps at the ten-day battle of El Alamein in early November. Later that month the 250,000 German troops around Stalingrad found themselves surrounded by Soviet forces. They surrendered in January despite Hitler's order that they should fight on to the last man.

GENOCIDE BEGINS

Once the war with Russia had begun, Hitler spent most of his time at *Wolfsschanze* (The Wolf's Lair), his base in east Prussia. As German armies pushed eastwards, Jews remaining in Germany were transported to the conquered areas and Jews already there were rounded up and killed. In January 1942 a conference in Berlin outlined plans for the mass murder of all Jews by the **SS**. Hitler left Heinrich Himmler to oversee this 'Final Solution'. Although there is no document directly linking Hitler's signature to the **Holocaust**, *Fuhrenwunsch* (Leader's Wish) was an established procedure of the Nazi regime. Hitler would simply let it be known that something should happen – and it did.

THE ROAD TO RUIN

In January 1943 the US President, Franklin D Roosevelt, and the British Prime Minister, Winston Churchill, agreed that they would fight on until Germany was forced to surrender completely. This reassured the Soviet Union that the USA and its **allies** would not make a separate peace.

'UNCONDITIONAL SURRENDER'

Although most opponents of the **Nazis** had been driven abroad or imprisoned in **concentration camps**, there were still secret plotters in Germany who hoped to overthrow Hitler and end the war by negotiating an agreement short of total surrender. The demand for 'unconditional surrender' made this idea seem hopeless but some plotters still thought they should try. At the end of 1943 Roosevelt, Churchill and Stalin agreed that after its defeat, Germany would be divided up and occupied by troops of the victorious nations.

'All alliances in history have fallen apart sooner or later … We will continue this battle until … one of our … enemies gets too tired to fight any more. We will fight until we get a peace which secures the life of the German people for the next 50 or 100 years, a peace which above all does not shame our honour a second time, as in 1918.'

Hitler, in a speech at a military conference, 31 August 1944

Hitler on his 56th birthday inspecting boy soldiers of the Hitler Youth Movement. Taken on 20 April 1945, it is one of the last photographs of him to have survived.

THE TURNING TIDE

In May 1943 the German Afrika Korps surrendered. In July the Allies invaded Italy. As Italian forces began to give up, Hitler was forced to send German troops to hold up the Allied advance.

In July 1943 the biggest tank battle in history took place around the Russian city of Kursk. The Germans lost 70,000 men, 1500 tanks and most of their aircraft. From then onwards, the war in the East became one long retreat for German forces as they were driven backwards.

On 6 June 1944, D-Day, came the invasion of northern France by Allied forces. Although German defenders failed to stop the Allies on the beaches they did fight back strongly, slowing up their advance. Hitler ordered all German men aged between 16 and 60 to form home defence units to support the regular army if Germany itself was invaded.

THE JULY PLOT

On 20 July 1944 Colonel Claus von Stauffenberg, a hero who had been badly wounded in the early part of the war, placed a bomb underneath the map table at Hitler's war headquarters and left, saying that he had to take a phone call. As he got away he heard the bomb go off and sent a signal to other plotters throughout Germany telling them that Hitler was dead.

'Who says I am not under the special protection of God?'
Hitler, after the failure of the July Plot, 1944

Hitler shows Mussolini (far left) the wreckage caused by the assassination attempt of 20 July 1944.

Although the bomb injured Hitler, it did not kill him, partly because the thick map table protected him and partly because the windows of the room were wide open because of the summer heat. This lessened the force of the blast. Hitler's survival convinced him – and many devoted **Nazis** – that however badly the war seemed to be going, he was bound to win in the end.

Hitler's revenge on the plotters was terrible. Anyone linked with them was hunted down. In all, some 7000 people were executed. The main leaders of the plot were strangled slowly with piano-wire.

IN A WORLD OF HIS OWN

Hitler had never believed that anyone who disagreed with him might be right. Generals who argued with him were simply dismissed. As the war situation got worse he ignored the facts, refusing to visit bombed German cities or read reports of defeats. When a train-load of wounded soldiers passed by his own railway-carriage once, he just drew the curtains to avoid looking at them. Hitler's health also began to fail badly. He relied on pills and injections to help him sleep or keep awake. At one time his doctor was giving him up to 28 different drugs a day. But Hitler still believed that, like a hero in a Wagner opera, he would triumph against all the odds through sheer genius and will-power.

The Last Days

Even after a surprise German fight-back in southern Belgium failed and Soviet armies launched a major advance in the east, Hitler still refused to admit defeat.

No surrender

Although he was increasingly ill and exhausted, Hitler kept tight control over both the **Nazi** party and the armed forces. He hoped that German scientists might still come up with a secret weapon that would completely turn the tide of the war. Hitler also hoped that Germany's enemies would quarrel, letting him make a separate peace with the USA and its **allies** while continuing to fight the **communist** Soviet Union. He also forbade any surrender by German troops, even when they were hopelessly outnumbered or surrounded. He believed that those who failed to bring him victory deserved only death.

Hitler's legacy – the **concentration camp** victims.

THE ALLIES CLOSE IN

On 30 January 1945, 12 years to the day since he came to power as Chancellor, Hitler made his last radio broadcast. By then he had been living underground in a concrete hideout in Berlin for a month. He was never to leave it again. On 19 March he ordered Germany's industries to be totally destroyed rather than fall into enemy hands. Albert Speer, the expert in charge of war production, managed to prevent this happening on a large scale. On 12 April President Franklin D Roosevelt died. Hitler hoped that under another leader, the USA might stop fighting. But there was no let-up in the pressure from the west or east. Four days later Russian troops fought their way into the suburbs of Berlin itself.

THE END

On 30 April Hitler married Eva Braun and immediately ordered her to take poison. Then he shot himself. Hitler had a deep fear that the Russians might seize his body and put it on public display. He had therefore ordered that his body be burned.

'The victor will not be asked afterwards whether he told the truth or not. In starting and waging a war it is not right that matters, but victory.'

Hitler, quoted by W L Shirer in
The Rise and Fall of the Third Reich

WHAT PEOPLE THOUGHT ABOUT HITLER

'Many of us … have a feeling that we are living in a country where fantastic hooligans and eccentrics have got the upper hand.'

Sir Horace Rumbold, British Ambassador to Germany, 1933

Hitler at a political rally in 1933, in Dortmund, Germany.

'What that ridiculous corporal says means nothing to us.'

Ernst Röhm, **SA** leader 1934

'I should be pleased, I suppose, that Hitler has carried out a revolution on our lines. But they are Germans. So they will end up ruining our idea.'

Benito Mussolini, **Fascist** leader, 1935

'Our leader (Hitler) said … " We have made human beings once more of millions of people who were in misery …" Anyone who will not deny himself a pound of butter for that is not worthy to be a German.'

Hermann Göring, Nazi leader, 1936

'Hitler is a monster of wickedness … in his lust for blood and **plunder**. Not content with having all Europe under his heel … he must now carry his work of butchery and desolation among the vast multitudes of Russia and of Asia. The terrible military machine, which we and the rest of the civilized world so foolishly … allowed the Nazi gangsters to build up year by year from almost nothing, cannot stand idle lest it rust or fall to pieces … '

Winston Churchill, British Prime Minister, speaking about the German invasion of Russia in 1941

An English translation of Mein Kampf.

'Hitler's dictatorship was the first … which employed to perfection the instruments of technology … Telephone, teletype and radio made it possible to transmit the commands of the highest levels directly to the lowest … where, because of their high authority, they were obeyed without question … . The instruments of technology made it possible to keep a close watch over all citizens and to keep criminal organizations hidden in secrecy…'

Albert Speer, Hitler's Minister for War Production, 1946

The August 1934 edition of a French **satirical** magazine. It shows Hitler with his head at the centre of a target, but he is in the traditional pose of a saint, complete with halo.

'His rise to power was not inevitable … yet there was no-one who equalled his ability to exploit and shape events to his own ends. … His originality lay in his methods rather than his ideas … By the time he was defeated, he had broken down the whole structure of the world in which he lived …'

Lord Bullock, British historian

'The Third Reich, which was born on 30 January 1933, Hitler boasted would endure for a thousand years. It lasted 12 years and four months, but in that flicker of time, as history goes, it caused an eruption on this earth more violent and shattering than any previously experienced … It is true that he found in the German people a natural instrument which he was able to shape to his own sinister ends. But without Adolf Hitler, who was possessed of a demonic personality, uncanny instincts, a cold ruthlessness, a soaring imagination and – until toward the end, when he over-reached himself – an amazing capacity to size up people and situations, there almost certainly would never have been a Third Reich.'

William L.Shirer, American journalist

'History will remember us as the greatest statesmen of all times or as her greatest criminals.'

Josef Goebbels, **Nazi propaganda** chief

Hitler in 1933 in Nazi uniform. Notice the Iron Cross on his pocket which shows he was decorated for bravery in the First World War.

ADOLF HITLER – TIMELINE

1889 (20 April) Hitler born at Braunau-am-Inn, Austria

1914 Hitler volunteers for the German army and is awarded the Iron Cross (2nd class)

1916 Hitler is wounded

1918 (11 November) Hitler is awarded the Iron Cross (1st class) and temporarily blinded in a gas attack
World War I ends

1919 (September) Hitler joins the National Socialist German Workers' Party.
Versailles **Treaty** signed

1921 Hitler becomes leader of the **Nazi** party and forms the **SA**

1923 German currency collapses
First Nazi party mass-meeting held, in Munich
French and Belgian troops occupy Ruhr industrial region
Failure of attempted seizure of power in Munich.

1924 Hitler serves eight months in prison

1925 Nazi party re-founded and **SS** formed
First volume of *Mein Kampf* published
Hindenburg elected president

1926 Second volume of *Mein Kampf* published

1927 Nuremberg becomes the centre for Nazi mass-meetings

1928 Nazi party wins 12 seats in the *Reichstag*

1929 Business crisis in USA and Europe causes trade collapse and mass **unemployment**

1930 Nazis win 107 *Reichstag* seats

1931 Collapse of German banking system.
Hitler's niece Geli Raubal kills herself in his apartment

1932 Hitler becomes a German citizen
Nazis win 230 *Reichstag* seats

1933 (30 January) Hitler becomes Chancellor (Prime Minister) of Germany
Enabling Law grants Hitler the powers of a **dictator** for four years
Nazis win 288 *Reichstag* seats.

1934 (30 June) SS murder SA leaders in the 'Night of the Long Knives'
President Hindenburg dies
Third **Reich** established with Hitler as *Führer* (Leader) – combining the offices of Chancellor and President
Army swears loyalty to Hitler personally

1935 Anti-Jewish Nuremberg Laws proclaimed
Compulsory military service is introduced

1936 Hitler orders the army to move back into the Rhineland, sends troops to support the **Fascists** in the Spanish **Civil War** and becomes an **ally** of Mussolini
Olympic Games held in Berlin

1938 Hitler becomes Commander-in-Chief of Germany's armed forces
Germany takes over Austria and the Sudetenland

1939 Germany takes over Bohemia and Moravia
Hitler agrees with the Soviet Union to divide Poland and conquers Poland
Rationing introduced in Germany
(3 September) Britain and France declare war on Germany

1940 Hitler conquers Belgium, Netherlands, Luxembourg, Denmark, Norway and France

1941 (11 November) Hitler invades Yugoslavia, Greece and the Soviet Union and declares war on the USA

1943 German army attacking Stalingrad surrenders
Italy surrenders to the Allies

1944 (6 June) Allies invade Normandy
(20 July) Hitler survives an attempt to kill him

1945 (30 January) Hitler makes last broadcast
(19 March) Hitler orders the total destruction of German industry
(30 April) Hitler kills himself in Berlin
(8 May) VE (Victory in Europe) Day marks the end of the war in Europe
(July) Allies meet at Potsdam, to organize the post-war occupation of defeated Germany

1949 German Federal Republic (West Germany) created out of US, British and French occupation zones. Soviet-occupied East Germany remains a separate **communist** state

1990 West and East Germany re-united

GLOSSARY

ally friendly nation acting as a partner

architecture the art of designing buildings

Aryan member of the highest racial group in the Nazi pyramid of human types. The word originally described a group of languages spoken in northern India from which both German and English have developed. Later the word meant people who spoke those languages. They were thought of as an ancient race of tough warriors of outstanding beauty and intelligence.

The language link is a matter of history. The idea of a heroic 'master race' has no basis.

Blitzkrieg (Lightning War) method of war using tanks, mobile artillery and planes to achieve rapid destruction of enemy forces

Bolshevik Russian communist

boycott refusal to buy from or deal with a person

civil war war inside a country over how it should be governed

coalition government made up of different political parties

communism the idea that a single ruling political party can run a country for all its people's benefit better than if they are left to make their own decisions and keep their own private homes, land and businesses. In practice communist governments have usually been cruel dictatorships.

concentration camp prison where political opponents could be concentrated together; in theory they were to be 'educated' through work and exercise; in practice, torture and murder was common

conservative believing in little change, and opposed to socialism and communism

democracy system of government based on the equal right of all citizens to speak on political matters and take part freely in choosing and changing their leaders

dictator ruler with complete power, not answerable to a parliament

fascism movement favouring inequality, leadership by a dictator

Führer leader

genocide deliberately organized mass murder of a people

Gestapo (*Geheime Staatspolizei,* Secret State Police) the most feared of Nazi security services, usually able to act outside the law

Holocaust The Nazis' murder of 6,000,000 Jews during the Second World War

Lebensraum (Living Space) territories to be conquered and settled by Germany

Luftwaffe (Air Weapon) the German airforce

Nazi short name of the National Socialist German Workers' Party (*Nationalsozialistische Deutsche Arbeiterpartei*)

negotiate settle a problem or dispute by talking; usually both sides agree to give up part of their demands

Nuremberg Laws racist laws taking away many political and legal rights from Jews

persecution deliberate ill-treatment

plunder steal by force

propaganda methods of publicity and persuasion using symbols and slogans to win support for a cause, party or person

reich realm

Reichstag the German parliament

reparations payments intended to make up for damage caused by war

republic system of government headed by an elected president rather than a king or emperor born to be a ruler

satirical something which uses humour to mock people or their faults

SA (*Sturmabteilungen*, Stormtroopers) private army of the Nazi party

SS (*Schutzstaffel*, Protective Wing) Hitler's bodyguard which expanded to become an army

socialism the idea that everyone should have an equal share of a country's wealth. Unlike communists, socialists accept democracy and changes of government by free elections

Soviet belonging to the Soviet Union (USSR)

strike refuse to work until a dispute, usually over wages or working conditions, is settled

swastika (*Hakenkreuz*) the official symbol of Nazism; based on an Indian design, associated with the ancient Aryans

synagogue Jewish place of worship

trade union organization to protect and improve the rights and interests of workers

treason the crime of trying to overthrow a government by force or other illegal methods

treaty official agreement between different countries

unemployment not having work

USSR (Union of Soviet Socialist Republics) an empire in which communist Russia controlled neighbouring countries from 1917 to 1991

INDEX